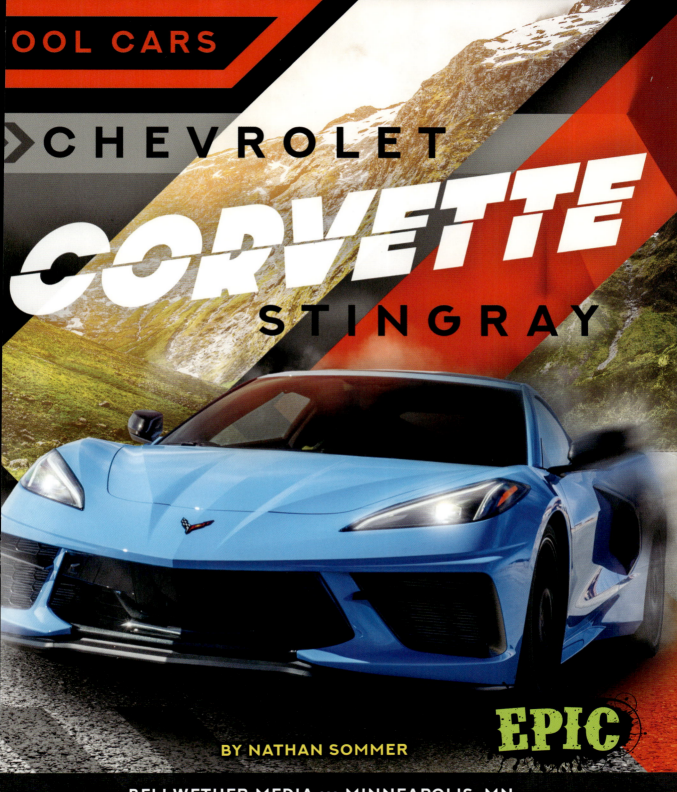

EPIC BOOKS are no ordinary books. They burst with intense action, high-speed heroics, and shadows of the unknown. Are you ready for an Epic adventure?

This edition first published in 2023 by Bellwether Media, Inc.

No part of this publication may be reproduced in whole or in part without written permission of the publisher. For information regarding permission, write to Bellwether Media, Inc., Attention: Permissions Department, 6012 Blue Circle Drive, Minnetonka, MN 55343.

Library of Congress Cataloging-in-Publication Data

LC record for Chevrolet Corvette Stingray available at: https://lccn.loc.gov/2022020244

Text copyright © 2023 by Bellwether Media, Inc. EPIC and associated logos are trademarks and/or registered trademarks of Bellwether Media, Inc.

Editor: Kieran Downs   Designer: Jeffrey Kollock

Printed in the United States of America, North Mankato, MN

TABLE OF CONTENTS

THE OPEN ROAD	4
ALL ABOUT THE CORVETTE STINGRAY	6
PARTS OF THE CORVETTE STINGRAY	12
THE CORVETTE STINGRAY'S FUTURE	20
GLOSSARY	22
TO LEARN MORE	23
INDEX	24

THE OPEN ROAD »

A Chevrolet Corvette Stingray coasts through the desert. The open road lies before it.

ALL ABOUT THE CORVETTE STINGRAY »

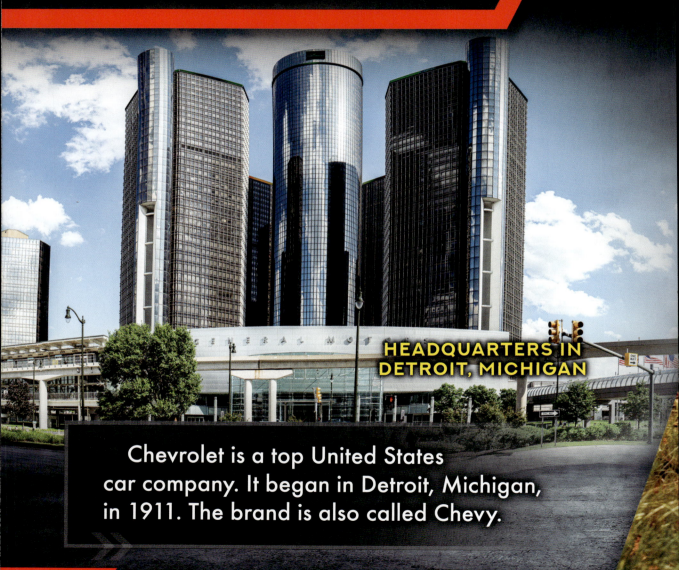

HEADQUARTERS IN DETROIT, MICHIGAN

Chevrolet is a top United States car company. It began in Detroit, Michigan, in 1911. The brand is also called Chevy.

Chevys are long-lasting. Popular **models** include the Silverado and Camaro.

2024 SILVERADO EV RST

MILLIONS OF CHEVYS
Nearly 18 million Silverados sold from 1998 to 2020!

The Corvette was first made in 1953. It was built for races. It went against British sports cars.

The Stingray **debuted** in 1963. Its body was brand new.

1953 CORVETTES BEING MADE

SHARK-INSPIRED
The first Stingray's body was modeled after a mako shark.

CORVETTE STINGRAY BASICS

- **YEAR FIRST MADE** — 1963
- **COST** — starts at $60,900
- **HOW MANY MADE** — 26,216 made in 2021

FEATURES

- 6.2L LT2 V8 engine
- low spoiler
- front splitter

9

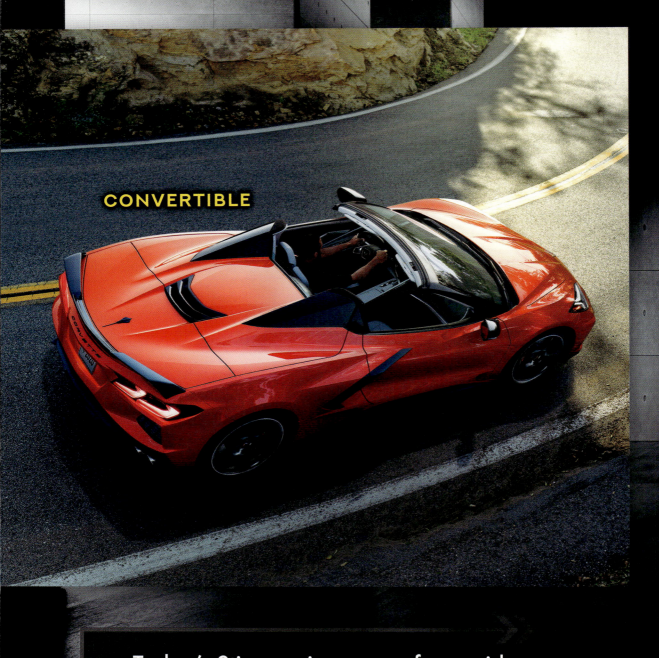

CONVERTIBLE

Today's Stingray is an even faster ride. It comes as a **coupe** or **convertible**.

The 2022 model is the most powerful yet. It speeds to 60 miles (97 kilometers) per hour in 2.9 seconds!

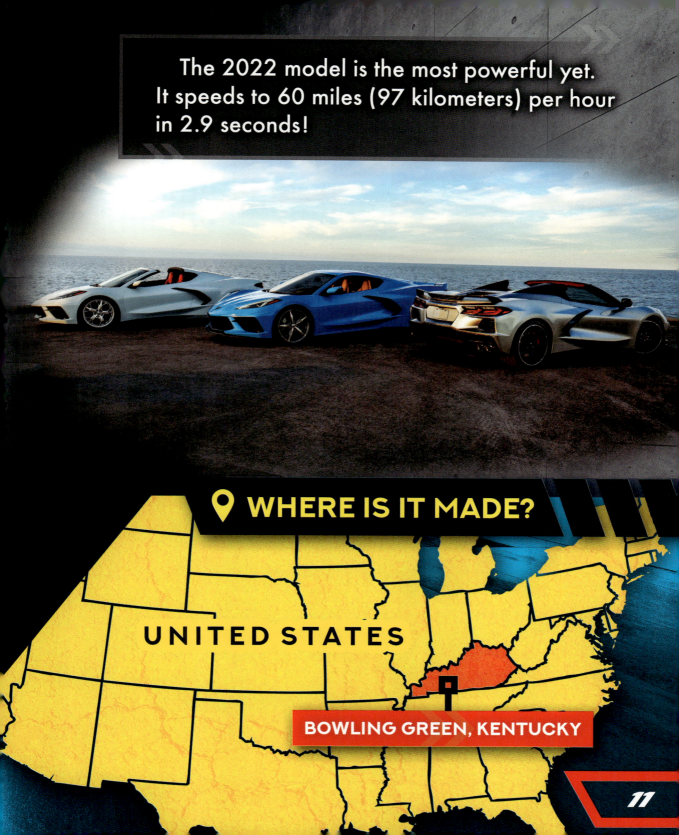

📍 WHERE IS IT MADE?

UNITED STATES

BOWLING GREEN, KENTUCKY

PARTS OF THE CORVETTE STINGRAY

The Stingray has a **V8 engine**. This powers it to speeds of 194 miles (312 kilometers) per hour. The engine sits behind the seats. This helps the car move around tight corners.

🛠️ ENGINE SPECS

6.2L LT2 V8 ENGINE

TOP SPEED — 194 miles (312 kilometers) per hour

0-60 TIME — 2.9 seconds

HORSEPOWER — 495 hp

The Stingray's body is made of **composite materials**. Deep **scoops** are found on each side.

SCOOP ›››

SIZE CHART

WIDTH — 76.1 inches (193.3 centimeters)

Convertibles have folding roofs.
Coupes have removable roofs.
They can be stored in the trunk.

The Stingray has a large touch screen inside. The car can have a heated steering wheel. It can also have heated seats.

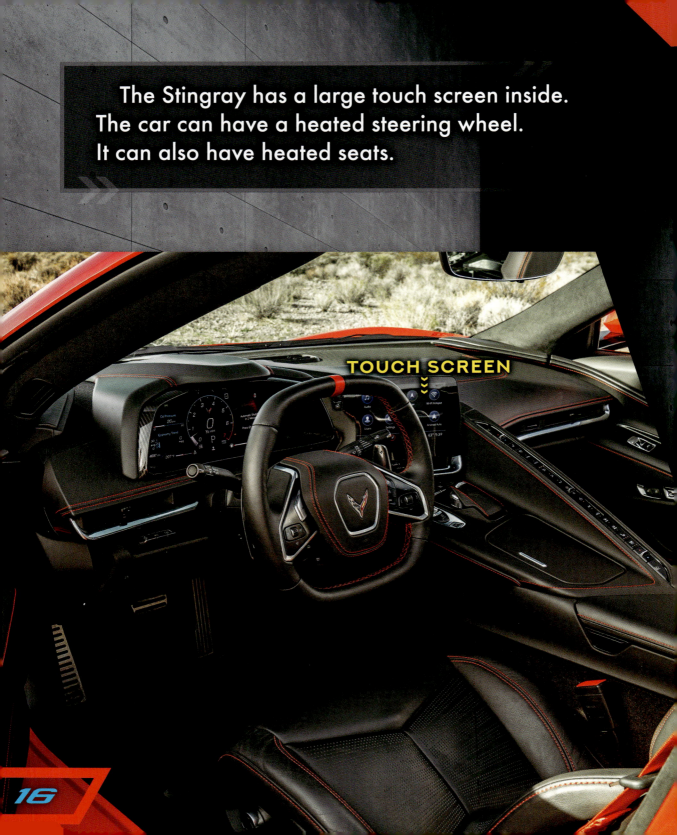

TOUCH SCREEN

CARGO SPACE

Two trunks provide extra **cargo** space. A 14-speaker **stereo system** is also available!

The Stingray has a low **spoiler** on the back. It also has a front **splitter**. These give the car smoother **handling**.

The car has different models. The C8.R is built after Chevy's winning race car. It has stripes and a racing **logo**!

ALL IN A NAME

The Corvette is named after a type of small warship.

C8.R

SPLITTER

THE CORVETTE STINGRAY'S FUTURE »

Chevy plans to keep making Corvettes. Chevy also plans to build an **electric** model. Future cars will be even more powerful.

The Stingray is one fast car. It is an American favorite!

FREE GUY

A Corvette Stingray was in the 2021 film Free Guy!

21

GLOSSARY

cargo—items carried by a vehicle

composite materials—materials made of two or more types of substances; composite materials are used to make things like cars.

convertible—a car with a folding or soft roof

coupe—a car with a hard roof and two doors

debuted—first came out

electric—powered by electricity; electric cars do not need gas to run.

handling—how a car performs around turns

logo—a symbol used to identify a brand

models—specific kinds of cars

scoops—parts on a car that control airflow to the engine

splitter—a flat scoop under the front bumper that helps a car move through air

spoiler—a part on the back of the car that helps the car grip the road

stereo system—an electronic system that plays audio such as music through speakers

V8 engine—an engine with 8 cylinders arranged in the shape of a "V"

TO LEARN MORE

AT THE LIBRARY

Borgert-Spaniol, Megan. *Chevrolet Corvette*. North Mankato, Minn.: Abdo Publishing, 2021.

Romaine, Claire. *Classic Corvettes*. New York, N.Y.: Enslow Publishing, 2021.

Sommer, Nathan. *Bugatti Chiron*. Minneapolis, Minn.: Bellwether Media, 2023.

ON THE WEB

FACTSURFER

Factsurfer.com gives you a safe, fun way to find more information.

1. Go to www.factsurfer.com.

2. Enter "Chevrolet Corvette Stingray" into the search box and click 🔍.

3. Select your book cover to see a list of related content.

INDEX

basics, 9
body, 8, 14
Bowling Green, Kentucky, 11
C8.R, 19
company, 6, 7, 19, 20
composite materials, 14
convertible, 10, 15
coupe, 10, 15
Detroit, Michigan, 6
electric, 20
engine, 12, 13
engine specs, 12
Free Guy, 21
handling, 18
history, 6, 7, 8
models, 7, 11, 19, 20
name, 19
racing, 8, 19
roofs, 15

sale
scoo
seat
size
spe
split
spo
stee
ster
touc
trun

The images in this book are reproduced through the courtesy of:
9 (isolated, engine, spoiler, splitter), 10, 11, 12 (engine), 12-13,
18-19 (left), 18-19 (right), 20-21 (left), 20-21 (right); J.A. Dunba